AURORA'S UNICORN

SIMONI KHETANI

ISBN 979-888546083-5

To my parents, my sister who encouraged me to write.

Dedicated to some of my close friends for always being the backbone for everything I do.

This book is dedicated to all the folks out there who find in love with nature as well as are in love with anyone

Contents

Contents

Preface

I am just an ordinary girl who occasionally has thoughts and ideas coming out of the blue. My mind is always thinking of some or the other thing that is the main reason why I love to write- so that I can capture the thoughts on paper before they disappear. I hope you enjoy reading my little poetry collection as much as I enjoyed it writing.

Poems here are on various subjects written at different times and prompted by very different feelings; but which will be read at one time and under the influence of one set of feelings. The sole purpose of publishing this book is to share my love of poetry with the world, and hopefully receive a kind response.

Acknowledgements

Writing my first book has been challenging as well as exhilarating, and I couldn't have done it alone. This book is the product of many people's support, motivation and dedication.

A big thank you to all! Special thanks to my family. Also this took a great motivation from my friends, so a big thank you to all of them. The professors NIFT-Gandhinagar as well all the teachers who taught me till now, it wouldn't be the same without them.

I would also like to give vastly appreciative thanks for making me take this step and support to my mother and sister - Suhani. They became the map to my journey, and I wouldn't have reached this destination without them.

Last but not the least, the reader, thank you for picking this book up. Hope you have a good read!

About The Author

Simoni Khetani is a writer, an engineer and to-be fashion technologist. She is based in Ahmedabad, Gujarat. Currently pursuing Masters of Fashion Technology from National Institute of Fashion & Technology (NIFT) – Gandhinagar. A few of her Poems have been published in anthologies published by Writer's Pocket and The Write Order.

Simoni enjoys reading short stories and poems. The first poem was written when she was in 10th grade. And then started writing poems since then. Loves to express the emotions through words. Apart from writing, she loves to paint and sketch. The best words that describe her are, enthusiastic, adventurous, fun-loving.

CHAPTER ONE

Seconds to Forget

A few short seconds can,
Lead you in a whole new direction.
The truth I hold,
Will take years to unfold,
Locked up and never told.
Two years passed on by,
I have no tears left to cry.
I escaped this hate,
No more videos left to tape,
Everyday that goes by,
I feel ashamed and left to die.
I still dream of running,
Of trying to break away,
Day and night,
Full of fright.
Those dark memories,
Still haunts my brain,
Every night I lie awake,
Wondering how much I can take.
And for once they will see,
They can no longer hurt me...

CHAPTER TWO

Patterns Of Life

Deciphering the maze
Of events with symbols
Like a maze that never ends
But can be found a way
Out by going in
Code of life
One graph at a time
Subtract toxic emotions
Multiply with good wishes
With the hues of experiment
Beat the contrasting demons
Transitioning and adapting
Impossible to replace
Delicate design with
Intricately woven patterns
Decorating our memories
In HEAVEN.

CHAPTER THREE

Coruscate

This shining light reflects my
Strength in times of despair
And make me feel I can

This shining light reflects my
Brightness in the darkest hour
In the mildest world

This shining light reflects my
Soul that its just so pure
To find another pure soul

This shining light reflects my
Aura, but there are shadows
That reveal my darker side

This shining light reflects my
Inner thoughts which are
sophistically rejected by society

This shining light reflects my
Soul and my inner peace
Which relaxes me so much

This shining light reflects my
Shining amour under the dark clouds
I'm a star shining persistently

CHAPTER FOUR

Night Hawk

Thoughts collide with beauty
Forms a dream
Glowing in the dark stars
Hooting with the breezes
Burning midnight oil
Soaring seamlessly
Staying sharp
Visionary of the light
Howling at the night
In dream world
There's still sound
In silence
With unheard rhythm
Darkness dancing around
With sparkle inside me!

CHAPTER FIVE

Embrace Elegance

He is her's,
She is his's.
Fights like Tom & Jerry,
Calls with weird names.
Gave each other,
Millions of names.
Millions is memories,
The time they spent.
Those messages,
That one,
Late night call.
From him to her,
Just to say,
Go to bed,
You are not well.
And then the journey started.
And ended too,
But not together.
Still their heart beat,
For each other.
When they see each other,
After a long time.
That glance,

Changes the smile,
One her face.
But he,
He doesn't even care.
And then,
Soon she gave up,
But still not in peace,
Not together!

CHAPTER SIX

Lane Of Reminiscence

Though we no longer see them
They are always in our thoughts
When sun rises each morning
Reminds me of their smile.

Those special memories
The gossips all night
The secrets to share
The things to scare

At that uneasy night
One call of yours
Turned my thoughts to us
And changed my darkness!

One smile of yours
Relieves all my pain
A trail of your thoughts
Gives a new reason to remember you...

CHAPTER SEVEN

The Lost Spark

Moon hides behind the clouds,
To smile again,
With a crescent curve.

The spark left me bewildered,
When it ignited an,
Evening meant to be shallow.

Somewhere down the road,
In the whispers of dried leaves,
There lies a silenced hope.

Somewhere along the way,
Roads are left behind,
And memories distort & decieve.

While we spun our lives,
We are forgetting our vines,
And running out of time.

As the years passed,
Will develop again,
Admist the closeness.

Butterflies died in my stomach,
For you took too long,
To bloom again.

I wished to re-ignite,
For the things,
I sparked for!

CHAPTER EIGHT

Power Of A Smile

Ceaseless wonders of the world
Flawless expression of every person
Effortless way of winning hearts.

Relaxes your mind
Soothes your heart
A cherished award.

Boycotts sadness
Becomes jovial
Eradication of nothingness.

Hatred vanished
Anger dismissed
Evacuated bitterness.

Simply but luxurious
Essential but priceless
Powerful but precious.

CHAPTER NINE

Fallen Leaves

Let the winds clear it
Let the sun burn it
They fall with a promise
That they will grow again
They'll spread their elegance again
When motion is the way of life
With each passing wind
And sound of leaves
Making noise realizes
Coming a new hope
Bidding a goodbye
With the new colors of happiness
Rejuvenating with the soil
Decorating the road not taken
Inspiring souls to fly
Each leaf has its own story
Teaching us art
Of living a peaceful life!!

CHAPTER TEN

Cycles

A story within a story
Roaming the streets
Holding your back
Freedom on wheels
Without engine
A paddle needs efforts
Running into mines
Digging deep the lines
Forming the loops
Keeps spinning on my mind
Peddling through time
Cycling on a rhyme
A dream within a dream
A soul within a body
A story within a story.....!!!!

CHAPTER ELEVEN

Magical Music

Sweet, gentle stream
Flows like blood
Magnifies, signifies
And glorifies
The rhythmic chords of
Of glorious tunes
Chained to rhythm of
Crescendo in melancholic muse
Calming the storm
Feeling the fog
Listen to murmurings
With melodious beats
Publishing memories
Marching rhythm
And haunting melody...

CHAPTER TWELVE

Propel

Waiting for red lights
Of life to turn into green.

Wind buffeting my hair
To those calm streets.

Empty road & thousands of thoughts
Digging deep into my mind.

Changing landscapes are like
Shelter for aching soul

Unleash the slope of rage
Feel the wind & feel the sky.

Driving back with life
Making a million thoughts.

CHAPTER THIRTEEN

Puzzles

Countless emotional pieces
Love to remain broken
Keeping you on your toes
Lost in arrangements
Fragmented in oblivion
Occupies the restlessness
Squeeze's the brain
Memories keep on turning
Tickles my mind
Creates and enigmatic
In the midst of chaos
Completing all incomplete complex
Superficial state of peace
Still searching for missed piece
That completes you!!!

CHAPTER FOURTEEN

Falling Winter

Winter, white and silver,
The pretty snowflakes,
Falling from the sky,
Fading, sleeping, slowing down,
On the wall and housetops,
Soft and thick they lie,
Filling all the air,
Look into the garden,
Where grass was green,
Now converted by snowflakes,
Not a blade is seen,
All look soft and white,
The bare black bushes,
Every twig is laden.

CHAPTER FIFTEEN

Fantasy Of Siesta

It's a drug,
It's a small death,
The more you leave,
The more it catches you.

The moment you close your eyes,
The living nightmares come,
The anxiety, the stress,
The problems all are gone.

The night is dark,
It's silence is deep,
Wishes met at midnight,
In the forest of my dreams!!!

CHAPTER SIXTEEN

Modern Loneliness

Machines in wrist bands
Earphones are the armor
Sliding down the memory lane.

Walking through the valleys of darkness
Caging on cyber
Blocking and unblocking the soul.

Socially active
Brain becomes less reactive
Stalking and creeping out.

Weeping around with everybody
Smiling together with no-one
Only together, we can survive.

Loud yet voiceless
Echo yet emptiness
Isolation and loneliness

CHAPTER SEVENTEEN

Nocturnal Ponder

Hold the key, to
Unlock the depth of desires.

Spitting bars of emotion,
Behind the shadows,
Lies blurred lines,
Mystery to decode.

Assimilating the thrill,
Dismantling the structure,
A preamble destruction,
Demonstrating own creation.

Drowsiness from daily log,
Chaos all over the mind,
Always more in less,
Wondering what's right!

CHAPTER EIGHTEEN

Garden Of My Mind

Full of intangible,
Yet tangible colors,
Flow without any warning.

Harbors roses in dark,
Fantasies of my knight,
In the world of expectations.

Holds a utopia,
For the rose to accept,
The power of its throne.

Words of wisdom,
Guide in times,
Away from judgmental cages.

Seems like a lonely island,
Surround by the ocean,
The dust of restlessness.

Above the soil of ignorance,
An alert mind sprouting,
Let it blossom again forever.

CHAPTER NINETEEN

Commitments

A word less understood
An act not a word
Fathomed by everyone
The oath not even listened
With balance motion and emotion
Scared at first
Calmed with trust
Building a castle of honesty
Tearing down your walls
Transform promise into reality
Reality into existence
Atrocity into tranquility
Infirmity into ability
Dream into life!!!

CHAPTER TWENTY

Yearn

Intense longing for simple dream
Cuddled up together
Covered in a blanket of hope
Yearn to travel
Across the valley of our
Deep dark confusions
Where rainbow touched the land
Just to escape the reality...

The bright stars light years away,
Clutching the memories
Strong impulse running through veins
Weeping soul yearned
By long conversations at night with you
Craving life, I met you
Escaping betrayal, I met you
Reviving myself, I met you...

CHAPTER TWENTY-ONE

Serendipity

We are two constellations
Booming to make our points meet
Glowing with different stars
Travelling to reach far.

Together can bond
Timeless conversations
One spreading darkness
Other being the rising sun.

Let the moon see us
See us getting close
Sparkling all night
Twinkling all day!

CHAPTER TWENTY-TWO

Nature's Beauty

Endless sky
Cotton clouds
Chirping birds
Engraved energy
Endowed simplicity
Endured love

Blue ocean
Deadly waves
Pleasant sound
Marvelous creation
Shimmering path
Beyond imagination

Crimson tides
Glint sun
Mere reflections
Mapping serenity
Designing positivity
Eliminating negativity

The waterfall
Hiding horizon

Blessing showers
Tricking drops
Splashing water
Whistling winds...

CHAPTER TWENTY-THREE

Incomplete Stories

Are waiting for that one
Who can complete them
By making a beautiful memory
Who could give it a way
Just waiting for "the one"
From bottom of a barrel
Longing to meet the seashore
But haven't found the way
Like clouds in the sky
Like the blowing winds
Not easily defined
Like the ebb of waves
Awaiting for the end
Is me and he!

CHAPTER TWENTY-FOUR

No Matter What...

You mean the world to me,
Nothing will ever come between us.
The sparkle in your eye,
The warmth of your skin.
No matter what anybody says and does,
You will always be in my heart.
The touch of your hand,
The smell of your hair.
Your kiss on my lips,
Your body near mine.
Forever and never,
Your spot will never be replaced.
The stroke of your touch,
The feeling inside.
The beating of your heart,
That we may never part.
You hold the key to my heart,
And you have since we met.
I will love you forever,
And no matter how much we fight,
Like I said I will love you forever,
NO MATTER WHAT!

CHAPTER TWENTY-FIVE

Sound Of Silence

Like a subtle symphony
In an orchestra of
Astray notions
This deafening silence
Like a bomb ready to explode

Emotions bottled up in
Thirst of losing
Quenched by mere friendship
Amidst the cacophony of chaos
Listen to the thumbing heart

Hustling through the crowd
Eeriness of everything
Pierces through my existence
Brings back my conscience
The voice of tranquility

Screaming whispers in my cerebrum
Roaring like a wave
Deep down in my cave
I still long for you
To gear together for

The sound of destruction of this silence!

CHAPTER TWENTY-SIX

Blushing Stars

A dreamy sky
Full of black dreams
Ocean twinkling
Sand greasing
We under the stars
Reflecting togetherness
Butterflies giggling in stomach
Fairies tailing overhead
Waiting for dawn
That orange ray to lighten
Our lives with hope
From reflection
To reality and beyond!

CHAPTER TWENTY-SEVEN

A Growing Love

I had a feeling,
That I can comprehend,
In my deepest thoughts you are,
More than just a friend.

Take my hand and lead my way,
Pour all your deepest thoughts,
Let your soft voice whisper softly in my ear,
All those lovely things I want to hear.

I wouldn't want to,
Rush us now,
As love we explore,
But there's a growing love inside,
That we just can't ignore.

Break the wails and enter my heart,
Unite the chains,
Hold my hand and let me out,
Release my soul deep within.

I think of you when we are,
Alone, I think of you and me,

Secrets to cover,
Right from the start.

Our relationship has grown so strong,
Where could we have went went so wrong,
You were there when I needed you
Now I am there for you to need me.

To me you will be fine,
I see the pain that is in your heart,
And sometimes I feel it too,
My love for you will stay the same,
Never will I forget your name.

By my side, you will stay always,
I think of you day by day,
I am ready now,
Take my hand;
And let the love begin.

CHAPTER TWENTY-EIGHT

Love @ 18

Love is not always blind
Going the distance
Destiny drives love
Beyond the dimensions...
Coffee and conversations
Two cups of coffee
Like and endless dream
A rose from heart...
Love in air
Hoping to die
Hug of death
One last time...

CHAPTER TWENTY-NINE

Art Of Awareness

To stay sane, I walk,
Towards the path of,
Brave and courage,
All through,
An open eye,
Sees through,
A wonderful soul,
Tranquilness of sea,
Weighing too much,
On my anxiety,
Know where to pause,
When minds too obvious,
Key to self mastery,
Let me remind you,
That life has,
Neither trails nor milestones.

CHAPTER THIRTY

Overbearing

Stop beating,
Around the Bush,
I‘m a storm,
People blame me always but,
It’s my eyes that reveals,
A heart full of love,
Yet no one accepts it.
Words become daggers,
Piercing the hearts,
Without stitching the wounds.
I let numbness,
Break free from,
Magnifying eyes,
I’m flooded with
The burden of,
Pleasing everyone for acceptance,
The weight of my past mistake
Weighing my deeds,
On judgement everyday,
Trying to curb my cravings,
For showing affection.

CHAPTER THIRTY-ONE

A Wise Owl Once Said...

Don't give up
Never let go
You are stronger than you think
And braver than you know
Your past doesn't define you
Learn to wait
Good things take time
Burn those bridges
And rise above the mediocrity
Keep your eyes on prey
Feet on ground
Mind on focus
Weaving tapestry of your life
Days are full of light
Amidst the vague and cryptic darkness.

CHAPTER THIRTY-TWO

Dear Ocean

Your greatness in depth
Is beyond imagination
Your calm vastness is amazing
The way you engulf the serene blue
Matching the azure skies
The secret inside the bubbles
Calm and poised
Searching in your reflection
Million waves of dreams
Hitting the feet's
Completely submerging me
To the magnificent horizon
Singing the song of glee
Churning the wheels of peace.

CHAPTER THIRTY-THREE

Moon Moments

Through the dark nights
To the bright lights
Stuck somewhere in between twilight
Beautiful yet reckless
Momentarily leaves breathless
Phases of gesture
An unraveling beauty
Hidden in light and dark
A light to satisfy soul
To make the broken
Feel the whole universe shining.

CHAPTER THIRTY-FOUR

Concrete Forests

Finding solitude in the
Midst of corner walls
Seems beautiful from outside
Painted with loneliness from inside
While the deep roots
Are rotten and mangled
Floor by floor, we create
Brick by brick, we build
Pillar by pillar, we stand
Lifeless and limitless cage
constructed walls of fallen jungles
On an animal graveyard
Poisoned the rivers
Waiting for remedial from heaven.

CHAPTER THIRTY-FIVE

Colorful Existence

Me being the
Amalgamation of various pigments
With a tint of green and sapphire
That makes life yellow and bright
Spreading shades of glee

Blue for the eternal azure
White for the eternal peace
Yellow for the bright future
Red for the love flame

Pinks of the evening sky
Purple for breaking the dusk
Violet for the lavender field
Black for showcasing all the classics

Orange expressing the emotions of sun
Brown securing the earth
Grey balancing the neutrality
Green enduring the growth

Painting the life with
Every hue and every ardour

Creating a kaleidoscope of motifs
For a magical soul like you!!

CHAPTER THIRTY-SIX

A Journey To Being Indestructible

A few short seconds can,
Lead you in a whole new direction.
The truth I hold,
Will take years to unfold,
Locked up and never told.
Two years passed on by,
I have no tears left to cry.
I escaped this hate,
No more videos left to tape,
Everyday that goes by,
I feel ashamed and left to die.
I still dream of running,
Of trying to break away,
Day and night,
Full of fright.
Those dark memories,
Still haunts my brain,
Every night I lie awake,
Wondering how much I can take.
And for once they will see,
They can no longer hurt me...

CHAPTER THIRTY-SEVEN

Moonlight Days

Musical mizzle heals the pain
Repulsive is the moon
Blistering is the sun
Gliding is the boundless sky
Clouds ornate the majestic soul
The orb of the moon
Enchanting an eyeshot
The galaxy as black as mascara
Crowded with sun
Sprawling light
Alluring charm like azure
Sparkling aura like stars.

CHAPTER THIRTY-EIGHT

New Bunch Of Happiness

A bundle of happiness
Lovely munchkin
Chubby cheeks
Puffed claws
Clinging to my fingers
Those radiant eyes
Sparkling the future
Tones of cuteness
A quick pain killer
With a killing smile
Those tears
Tear me apart
Soft teddy
With a life in it
I would hug all day!

CHAPTER THIRTY-NINE

Illusions

Passes with reflections
Dodging deflections
Sledging the reflections

When its hard to explain
A corollary of emotions
Accept the false hypothesis

Eloquent silence of two
Louder than thunder
Can destruct mountains

Diminishing in a trap
Of endless pursuit
Already stuck in time dilation

Minutes are rolling
Gone with the gushing wind
Turning things surreal

And with this
Fantasies are created
With the exit of illusions...

CHAPTER FORTY

Musings

Falling out of reality
Creating own's hallucination
To imprison my monsters

Gazing out of the window
Just looking for the stars
To decorate the day sky

Vanishing into indigo night sky
Carrying the fragrance
Leaving the footprints

In a very dim light
Words couldn't reach
Darkened silence of yours

Birds dirge about
Daunting morning
Hiding sunrise beneath those wings

Losing ourselves to
Our mundane existence
For we are mere atoms!

About The Poetic Souls Publication

Poetic Souls is writers community, where we grow together while helping each other.

Motivation and ideas is what we all seek and give. Prompts, Challenges and various activities help a writer to think beyond the box and helps in their overall development.

Apart from this we also provide an author platform which encourages budding writer's to enhance their skills and make their work, reach a target audience of potential readers. ...

Its a growing community of the writers, managed by Rohan Nath and Nidhi Shukla.

9 798885 460835

Printed by Libri Plureos GmbH in Hamburg, Germany